Meet Me at the Farmers Market

Lisa Pelto

Illustrated by
Paula S. Wallace

To my daughters, Ellie and Monica, who showed me how to see the world through fresh eyes.

Special thanks to Ellie Godwin, Debra Ozment, Debra Pelto, and Paula Wallace who shared their extraordinary talents to make this book possible.

SECOND EDITION, 2019

Paperback ISBN: 978-1-945505-44-7
Hardcover ISBN: 978-1-945505-45-4
Mobi ISBN: 978-1-945505-46-1
EPUB ISBN: 978-1-945505-47-8
Library of Congress Control Number: 2019939037
Cataloging in Publication data on file with the Publisher.

ReadingIsKey@conciergemarketing.com
Reading is Key Publishing is a division of Concierge Marketing Inc.
For more information, visit www.conciergemarketing.com
Illustrations by Paula S. Wallace, www.paulawallacefineart.com

Printed in the United States of America
10 9 8 7 6 5 4 3 2

For all the growers and
farmers who bring us fresh,
local food each week.

Hi! My name is Sophia
and I'm seven years old!

My favorite part of the week is the weekend because that's when we go to the Farmers Market.

"Grab the grocery bags and let's go!" Mom says.

There are lots of people at the Farmers Market.
They come to buy fresh, local food and goods.

It's extra fun when I meet my friends there.

My friend Ava loves to cook.
I love exploring the market.
Noah has his own garden,
and Logan just loves to eat.

Mom calls us four peas in a pod!

Shoppers come with bags, baskets, bins, and lots of babies in buggies. Some people bring tiny dogs in strollers to our Farmers Market!

ALL NATURAL
FOR
DOGS AND PEOPLE

We listen to musicians
sing their hearts out right
in the middle of everything.

11

Fresh Carrot
Beets
Tomatoes

Kale
Lettuce
Potatoes

There are tables heaped with freshly picked vegetables and trucks piled to the sky with sweet corn.

12

We buy vegetables
and other foods
that are grown
close to our town.

13

Some vendors sell meat, cheese, and eggs.

Mom always tells Farmer Dan,
"Your eggs are the freshest, and that's no yolk!"

Farmer Dan says, "You crack me up!
See you next week."

Local farmers sell different foods as the seasons change.

I like the shiny, colorful peppers.

Logan loves summer when he can eat carrots all the time!

Ava can't wait for late summer when the melons are ready to eat.

18

Noah says fall is
the best because
he loves to carve
pumpkins.

We go to the Farmers Market
every week, rain or shine!

20

We visit Farmers Markets in faraway places when we go on vacation.

It's fun to try foods we don't find at our local Farmers Market. On one trip, I even tasted dragon fruit!

Violet, the gardener, tells
me how the wind, rain,
and sunshine help fruits
and vegetables grow.

24

Annie the beekeeper says, "Bees make the honey we eat, plus they help plants grow."

On some days we get yummy treats, like popsicles, lemonade, or roasted corn on the cob.

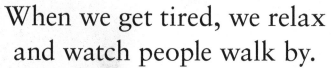
When we get tired, we relax
and watch people walk by.

I love going to the Farmers Market.
I hope to meet you there soon!

For more information

or to find your local Farmers Market,
visit these websites:

www.LocalHarvest.org
www.FarmersMarketCoalition.org

Lisa Pelto has been a publishing consultant for over three decades. She founded Concierge Marketing Publishing Services in 2004, and has helped hundreds of people reach their dream of becoming published authors. She teaches a popular writing and publishing series at the local community college, and presents her stories to elementary school children. Lisa and her family enjoy exploring and supporting their Farmers Markets in Omaha, Nebraska, and wherever they travel.

Artist and illustrator Paula S. Wallace has a studio in the Hot Shops Art Center in Omaha, Nebraska. Wallace, a graduate of the University of Iowa, enjoys illustrating for other authors, as well as writing and illustrating her own books. Wallace's work as a fine artist includes many gallery exhibits in the United States and Italy. Her book, *Choose Your Days*, was the sole selection to represent Nebraska at the 2018 National Book Festival in Washington, DC.

CPSIA information can be obtained
at www.ICGtesting.com
Printed in the USA
LVHW071908200723
752689LV00087B/175

9 781945 505454